Raising A Puppy
Handbook

The Art of Positive Puppy Training
Have a Well-Behaved Dog for Life

Written by
Michael Bronn
Lisa Manning

Copyright © 2013 Michael Bronn & Lisa Manning

All Rights Reserved. No portion of this book may be reproduced, stored in a retrieval system, or transmitted in any form or by any means – electronic, mechanical, photocopy, recording, or any other – except for brief quotations in printed review, without the prior permission of the publisher.

This publication is designed to provide accurate and authoritative information in regard to the subject matter covered. It is sold with the understanding that the publisher and authors are not engaged in rendering legal, accounting, medical or other professional advice or services. When any professional advice or other expert assistance is required, the services of a competent professional person should be sought.

Published by Water Street Press Publishing
2808 Olympia Drive
Grand Prairie, TX 75052

First Printing, 2013

ISBN-13: 978-0615883366
ISBN-10: 0615883362

Printed in the United States of America

"Whoever said you can't buy happiness forgot little puppies."
- Gene Hill

Did you get your FREE copy of my book? Just go to this link on the internet and you'll get all the extras as my gift. ($14.95 value)

"How To Care For Your Dog - 37 Proven Lessons"
http://www.m8u.org/PuppyLessons/

Table of Contents

INTRODUCTION 5

HOW TO SOCIALIZE YOUR PUPPY THE RIGHT WAY 11
    Initial Socializing Experiences 17
    Unvaccinated Puppy 20
    Puppy Introductions 21
    Discourage your puppy from biting. 23
    Get Your Puppy Familiar with Sounds 24
    Socializing With Your Friends 25
    Always Watching You with a 6th Sense? 26
    Children at the Park 29
    How to Reward Your Puppy 30
    Puppy School 34

HOW TO TEACH THE MOST IMPORTANT PUPPY SKILLS 39
    Heel 41
    Establish yourself as the pack leader 46
    Crate Training 55
    Puppy's Name 59
    Leash 63
    Socialization 66
    Visiting the Veterinarian 68
    No/Stop 70
    Come 71
    Sit 72
    Puppy Doors 76
    Control Biting 78

HOW TO CONQUER DIFFICULT TRAINING MISTAKES EVERY PUPPY OWNER MAKES 81

HOUSEBREAK YOUR PUPPY IN 7 DAYS USING THESE PROVEN 8 STEPS 95

CONCLUSION 107

Introduction

Is there anybody you know who really does not love puppies?

When things aren't going just right, all I need to do is turn to my puppies and the world is good again.

I started training puppies years ago, when I saw my best friend's brother give trouble to my friend's thirteen-pound, Jack Russell terrier. For some reason, the brother liked to intimidate this puppy as his method of greeting. He would stomp his foot to scare her, or jump in her way while loudly yelling her name. As she ran close to him, he would yell her name at the top of his lungs, "TIMMS!"

This all appeared to be playful experiences to the brother. However, what he was really doing would not be made clear for yet another a year.

When I was not around, the brother kept acting out his antics. I decided I wanted to be the exact opposite type of friend to this fun loving puppy.

I told myself that I wanted never to give this beautiful terrier a reason to fear me, to doubt me, or to question my motives in any way. I would never hit her, yell at her, make startling noises to get her attention, take food from her, or lock her away in dark, secluded rooms.

I wanted to earn her love and trust, while I gave her mine.

TIMMS was a young puppy, when I first started visiting, but not too young. My friend didn't know her real age, because friends in another city gave her to him. She was a constant barker, that sang loudly out of harmony with her sister all day long. Terriers are known for barking together when they get together, but that is just one trait to work on when a puppy is young.

The previous owners did not, so this puppy already had bad habits, and from the previous owners' training methods, TIMMS understood the swat of a hand.

I would extend my hand out to pet this puppy and watch it cower. Nothing gets my dander up more than when I see a puppy who has been mistreated in that way.

Many of TIMMS bad habits simply never showed up without her sister leading her. She was a new girl at this new house, and TIMMS was very receptive to kindness that she had not experienced before.
TIMMS would sometimes cry as we left the house. Of course, that separation anxiety is common, but she had found gentleness in my

friend and great comfort in all those who visited except the brother.

I learned to calm her by spending a little time with her before we left. Sometimes she would get a brief walk before I arrived, and in the beginning, we would leave for a few minutes and happily return to comfort her once again.

In a matter of days the crying stopped. TIMMS seemed comfortable and now happy in her new home.

I loved this puppy. It was clear she loved me back. Isn't that a great feeling to treat a part of life so well that the trust and love returned is genuine?

As the year continued, my friend would buzz me in through the front gate. TIMMS would hear the buzz through the phone, run out the open house door and race to me before I rounded the last corner. She usually won. When she saw me, she would jump into my arms and nuzzle my neck to say hello. I swear little TIMMS had wings, because I am tall and she jumped from many feet away and landed in my arms every time.

One day a group of us was meeting at my friend's house. I was running late, so I called. At the same time, there was a buzz at the gate. TIMMS bounded for the door and ran as fast as she could to get to the corner just as the brother stepped into view.

On sight alone, TIMMS loudly yelped, skidded to a stop as she ran back into the house.
The brother was ashamed. From then on, he tried to gain her trust and love, but TIMMS never would give that to him.

Just before the winter holidays a year later, my friend passed on from an accident. His family moved and took TIMMS with them. I did not see them for almost another year. When I walked into their house, TIMMS wailed loudly at me, made a mess on the floor and begged me to pick her up. The family said they had many people come and go during the year, but never did TIMMS react that way with anyone else. That was a magnificent reward to me for having loved TIMMS so easily. Some breeds need more assertiveness than other breeds, but I was never aggressive with TIMMS.

That entire experience created my philosophy on Training Puppies that I describe in this book.
  Michael Bronn

How to Socialize Your Puppy the Right Way

Training your puppy to be social means you are teaching your puppy how to be a good member of society. You help mold your puppy's actions and familiarize your puppy to the ways considered good behavior.

Socializing means that you are introducing your puppy to various types of people, sounds, smells, textures, and the many different experiences your puppy can absorb now within your controlled handling. The more varied experiences your puppy can have now with you at his side will make your adult puppy a peaceful and accepting animal.

Socialization starts the process of understanding the world without every situation becoming a startling adventure. The difference that this training provides is to help the puppy learn why Joe with a beard is a good friend, and the guy with a beard breaking in the front door is a hazard.

Unnecessary barking, biting, bad potty manners, jumping on friends and other actions not considered appropriate at specific times are the types of actions mostly easily correctable now.

Important:
The very good news is that the character of a puppy is adaptable. You can most easily mold that character when the puppy is very young, so start now. When your puppy is about 12 weeks old, your puppy will have determined how it chooses to respond to other animals, people, things and experiences. After 6 months, changing a response is much more difficult than creating a new response.

Your puppy can become bold or introverted, friendly or unreceptive, aggressive or passive or be just as helpful or troublesome like your next-door neighbor. Your puppy may have a combination personality of various traits and that makes your puppy unique.

Different character traits that establish the adult puppy's personality are determined by these primary factors:

1) to what extent your puppy has been socialized
2) type of breed
3) how you socialized your puppy.

Different breeds certainly have reputations for specific aggressive or docile traits, but these traits are not necessarily the greatest contributing factor to an adult puppy's personality. A German Shepherd can become a loving puppy, because it has been socialized with many other loving people and gentle puppies. However, these snap shots of a puppy's life can change as the puppy encounters different people and experiences as he grows older.

Socialization brings out the traits you desire. For example, Doberman's can be highly protective, single-family guard puppies when they are only exposed to the family and placed alone in a closed room when company comes over. Eventually that association can create a very protective animal that could be dangerous to visitors.

Primary traits are strongly reinforced depending on how you socialize your puppy. The heavy handed, loud voice methods can create puppies that obey out of fear. That does not mean they make good guard puppies or trusting family puppies. It just means they will do what you want until another avenue of change opens before them that does not rule them with a threat.

I grew up with an Airedale terrier. That stately member of the family was loyal and protective to every member of the family, but especially to my mother. My brothers and I would often tease my mother and get a little rowdy. Once, when we were getting a little too rowdy with my mother, the Airedale slowly walked between my mother and my brothers, while he was puffing his chops and looking sideways at us.

This was a confusing experience for the puppy, but we praised him for protecting my mother. We involved him in the fun at a less intense level. My mother was often home alone, and this caring dog made us all feel good knowing she had a powerful Airedale ready to defend her.

Your puppy can learn to remain calm and attentive to you as he grows older, because you gave the time necessary to expose your puppy to different weather, noises of cars and trucks, children that may come running up to play.

The key word here is DIFFERENT. In the weeks to come, after reading the rest of this book, take your puppy to parks and sports facilities where new noises and movements can become learning experiences to understand. Bring your puppy outside when the lawn mower is running or the family is making much splashing in the pool. Bring along some food treats as rewards that reinforce your positive verbal approvals.

Read the rest of this book before taking your puppy out with other dogs and noisy groups. Starting these activities is important, but they take a little planning for different reasons that are explained later on.

Most adult puppies are not properly socialized. You can easily see puppies that break away from their owners when a squirrel climbs up a tree or they go chasing a child on a tricycle.

By exposing your puppy to these experiences when it is young and in a safe environment with you, the puppy will naturally lose the need to bolt away as an adult to experience something it has already seen.

Initial Socializing Experiences

Right after you get your puppy home, your next step is to socialize your new addition during his initial stages. The sooner you train your puppy the better it will be for your puppy and you. It is easier to train a puppy that is just 3 to 12 weeks old as his experiences affect how he is adapting his personality that will remain with him throughout his life.

Between the ages of three and twelve weeks, a puppy will be most sensitive to socializing practice, meaning that any positive links he has with others will make an impression for life.

At this age, the outside world is not a safe place for your puppy. Not only can he not defend himself easily, he is not as resistant to possible harmful infections as he will be later in his life.

It's still important to get your puppy outside, but you must be aware of potential hazards that could create a problem. For the first few weeks, keep your puppy within very safe surroundings, mainly your home and your fenced in backyard or garden.

So, his socialization at this point will be restricted to linking with only those people and other animals that are living with him in the same house. That socialization will make you and your family the most important people in his life for a long time. The trust he builds for this nuclear group is dependent upon the loving relationships that are created by each member of the family.

Create a puppy exposure chart that starts out like this:

Age in Weeks:	8	9	10	11	12	13	14	15	16	17
Babies										
Noisy Children										
Teenagers										
Elderly										
Men - quiet, noisy, beards, hats										
Women - flowing dresses, high hair										
Loud crowds										
Different pets										
Delivery person with packages										
Vaccum cleaners, wash machines										

There are 1000's of different types of exposures you can use to help socialize your puppy. List as many as you can and expose your puppy to as many as you can before adulthood.

Be Prepared: Always think ahead how you might expect your puppy to react and how you will choose to handle the situation.

You can't learn from a book how to manage every experience that might arise. However, you can improve your own skills on how to respond to them.

Practicing in your mind what you think could happen in any socialization will help you be prepared. Eventually you will know your puppy better than any expert or guru trainer, because you and your puppy are unique.

Did you sign up for your free book? Just go to this link on the internet and you'll get all the extras as my gift.

"How To Care For Your Dog –

37 Proven Lessons"

http://www.m8u.org/PuppyLessons/

Unvaccinated Puppy

It can be risky to train a puppy that has not been vaccinated, but that does not mean you should wait to start socializing. If you wait to get all the shots before starting to socialize, your puppy will miss very important times to easily adapt to the world.

Be extra cautious of possible health risks. For example, socializing around other well-behaved puppies is important and helpful at this time, especially since you get to select this group of influence.

You can walk with other friends' puppies that are already well-trained. This is not a good time to take the puppy to a puppy park, where too many behavioral and disease unknowns exist.

Comfortable Relationships

Socialization at this point will not be difficult with people. Most people love puppies and puppies are just starting to discover a world that is unfolding. However, problems can develop when you try to socialize your puppy with other animals before your puppy is ready to make that leap.

At this stage, your main goal is for you first to establish a very good relationship with your puppy. Obedience to simple commands is what we have in the plan.

Your puppy's focus will be on you for the first few days before involving him with outside animals.

Puppy Introductions

The best clue to obtain successful socialization with other animals is to expose your puppy to as many different people and things as early as possible. It's important to socialize your puppy with other animals, as well, so your adult puppy will not be one of those leash pullers and barkers when he sees another four legged animal of any different type. The time to discover those animals safely is now.

Different animal motivations are not always what people may think. The puppies usually tend to attack the cats, and therefore it's important to create a good relationship among them.

Puppies are not always out to harm a cat, but instead find great curiosity in this different creature. Puppies and kittens still have an understanding instinct that they are both different, but as long as the puppy does not fear the kitten, you can more easily socialize your puppy with this different animal.

Simple methods like distracting your puppy's attention onto yourself, while you carry your puppy to the kitten are recommended.

Distraction can be a useful technique, but that technique works better when the kitten and the puppy are equal in size and temperament.

Socializing to different animals can create unexpected experiences depending on age.

Discourage your puppy from biting.

Play with your puppy as any puppy would play with him. Tickle him or wrestle with him. When your puppy bites you while playing, become serious and ignore his attempts to continue playing. This will help him to understand that it is not a good thing to bite anyone, another animal or person. As you read further into this book, you will learn about your role as the Pack Leader. The mother of your puppy would play with him, but she wouldn't tolerate him biting her. For puppies that just aren't getting the idea to stop biting, you can add 'NO/STOP' once this command is learned, and also 'SIT' while you ignore your puppy for a few minutes.

Get Your Puppy Familiar with Sounds

Often a puppy is very fearful when he hears loud noises for the first time. Your task is to help him become familiar and calm with unusual noises.

Make him listen to doorbells, banging pots and pans, sharp and cracking sounds, opening and closing car doors and horn noises that you control in the house and around your backyard. Gently show your puppy the world with a fun and attentive tone of your own. These aren't fearful sounds. They are just sounds.

After a few days, your puppy will stop reacting to these sounds as new experiences. Each week I like to add a few other sounds and come back to some of the others on my list.

An enjoyable experience awaiting you, is when you have trained your puppy to come to you by your call, and the puppy doesn't take its eyes off you even when an unexpected noise occurs.

Socializing With Your Friends

Instead of socializing your puppy with any strange puppy, try to socialize him with any of your friends. After your puppy has learned to manage friends, introduce your puppy to your friend who might have a puppy. As young of age as three to six weeks, your puppy is ready to go out of the house and meet other puppies. The age to leave the house depends upon the type and size of your puppy.

Your puppy might become frightened or growl upon seeing your friend. Calm your puppy down, and help him to see that your friend is no threat to you or him.

Walk your puppy in to the area where your friend is sitting. (Later approach your friend while he is standing.) Hold the leash tightly and slowly move towards your friend. Do not rush this, so your puppy does not get overly excited. Touch your friend's hand, as with a handshake, or touch your friend's arm, while the two of you have a gentle conversation. Move closer while being quiet as you observe your puppy.

Your puppy is learning more about the world and your friend is a new addition. Your puppy will respond to these new experiences partly based on how you manage yourself.

Always Watching You with a 6th Sense?

As part of the pack animal mentality, puppies are looking toward the pack master for that leadership. Your puppy is always watching you. Your puppy has its senses keenly aware of what is going on about him more than the average human thinks.

Your reactions and even silent emotions that it can sense, affect your puppy and how it will react during socializing situations. So, as you move and make decisions about your day to day experiences, your puppy is learning from you.

Most pet owners believe their pets have a sixth sense as reported in the Huffington Post from a poll conducted by GfK Roper Public Affairs and Corporate Communications.

"Now two-thirds of American pet owners say they can relate – their pets have a sixth sense about bad weather...."

Seventy-two percent of dog owners said they've gotten weather warnings from their pets...."

"Jim Fulstone says his farm dog, a Pomeranian named Austin, gives warnings about 15 minutes before earthquakes and 45 minutes before thunderstorms

"He'll run around in circles and look at you. If you sit down, he'll sit down with you. If you are outside, he will come up to you, run around, look off, sniff your leg, just kind of be there. He's a lot more active," said Fulstone, 65, of Wellington, Nev. "For the quakes, he was very alert and started barking and doing his run-around routine."

http://www.huffingtonpost.com/2011/01/11/pets-sixth-sense_n_807249.html

Puppies are always in tune with you as the pack leader. They are watching to understand what is expected of them. When they receive consistent and caring instruction, they are happy puppies.

Children at the Park

The first walk you have with your puppy that takes you near children at the park is most often a good memory. Your puppy is looking at a group of people that are a little closer in size to him. Imagine living in a world with a view from eight inches off the ground. Now walk up to a size 15 shoe. That's my shoe size. I purposely keep a step back from smaller animals who have actually barked directly at my shoes. I think they recognize them as one of their own. That may not be true, but that world around them is so different from what it first appears.

As your puppy gets vaccinated and is socialized more and more with other animals and people by your choosing, he will become ready for the park.

The first time or two you take your puppy to the park do not get too near any crowd. Observe from a distance, especially until after your puppy has received vaccinations. Watch how your puppy reacts to the crowd movements and the many different noises and scents that you may not even be able to hear or smell.

Your puppy's environment is expanding again and on many more invisible planes than what any of us can know.

Walking your puppy around various types of crowds helps your puppy understand that the people in the park are no harm to him. This is just a start.

Each time you return and when the time is right after vaccinations, introduce your puppy to groups.

How to Reward Your Puppy

Motivating your puppy when he accomplishes a goal or shows a positive attitude toward your friends and their pets is what helps your puppy know what is good for him to do. There are many types of positive reinforcement methods from treats to electronic devices to hugs and kisses.

The first important item to remember is that too much of one type of a reward can make the puppy only want to act because of the specific reward. Use rewards to reinforce the desirable action, but *the reward is not to become the single reason for the action.*

As you start training, it is important to use strong rewards frequently, but eventually use them 50% to 75% of the time as the puppy gets older.

I use the clicker method at times followed by a small treat.

The clicker method is helpful for me, too, because I have a speaking problem from time to time. It helps me maintain a consistent sound when my voice just won't do it.

I still want the puppy to respond to my voice, so I train with my voice when I can, but this is how I use the clicker and treats. It is best to choose one method, voice or clicker, through to completion, so you do not confuse your puppy.

To easily train your puppy to act in response to the clicker, use the following steps:

First, make sure your puppy has not eaten recently and is calm. (This is true for the start of most training sessions.)

Move to a quiet area so his attention can remain with your training. Have your supplies ready: pocket full of puppy treats and a clicker.

Click the clicker and then follow the sound right away with a treat. At this point, you are training your puppy to associate the clicker with the treat, so repeat this a few times.

Then wait for things to settle down while your puppy's attention is on something else.

Click the clicker.

Did your puppy give you his attention and want a treat?
No? Then continue reinforcing the clicker and the treat.
Yes? Then you are ready to train your puppy the basic commands coming up in the next chapters.

Puppy Training Clickers are inexpensive and are one of the easiest ways to help reward.

Remember to give plenty of loving praise. The clicker will make training easier by associating good behavior with a treat quickly, but your puppy will always want your love and attention more.

Puppy School

Getting out of the house is an important step. There are many items outside the house that a puppy may see as risky. There is much to discover that will be many times larger than what is found in the house. However, socializing outside the house can be fun. After your puppy has been vaccinated, he is probably ready to meet other puppies.

New puppy owners agree that one of the best places to introduce a puppy to other puppies is at Puppy School.

Your puppy will establish a good relationship with other puppies of his own species and many of which already have some training experience.

Puppy School also gives your puppy an opportunity to interact with other young puppies of different breeds. This additional socialization will help him see other puppies as a friend he already recognizes, instead of seeing other animals as new creatures that create excitable interests. Once your puppy understands that other animals are just another part of life, you will have a new level of trust in how your puppy will handle future situations that many other dogs won't manage well.

Puppy School interactions help develop a more poised dog that can learn to be calm even when other dogs are acting out.

Although Puppy Schools introduce puppies to other puppies in a positive environment, they also play a vital role in building good relationships between your puppy and other human beings.

An essential lesson your puppy will learn from other well-trained dogs is how to remain with other animals without biting.

When you see a puppy in your neighborhood that bites other puppies, you can be sure that he did not learn proper biting manners by playing with other puppies in puppy school.

Nipping during play is natural, but your young puppy will learn in puppy school that when he bites too hard and causes pain, then the puppy he has bitten will not want to play with him any longer.

Good biting manners today will expand into a puppy's relationships with people in the future.

It is important to socialize your puppy with others as this will help your pet understand how to act around other people and other animals for most of his life.

Puppy owners find socializing a puppy in respectable groups often funny, but an interesting goal to accomplish.

Puppy socialization helps your puppy to become a good and obedient dog and Puppy School is an extra bonus worth considering..

How to Teach the Most Important Puppy Skills

Owners should start training their new puppies as soon as they bring them home.

It is much easier to develop good traits in young puppies as opposed to teaching older puppies or dogs new tricks to change already developed bad habits.

At first, it can be difficult, and somewhat frustrating, when dealing with a puppy. However, the result of a well-behaved and happy puppy is worth the extra quality time you put into training.

.

Many owners have different ideas of what key skills should be taught puppies in their first year, but in most cases they are all looking for an instantly well-behaved pet. Training takes time because some breeds grasp different concepts easier than other breeds. Even so, reinforcing successful training days and weeks after is always worth putting into your plan.

That means that once a puppy has mastered walking calmly on a leash as other dogs walk by, reinforcing this excellent behavior every few weeks in your training session helps keep that successful action fresh in mind.

Young animals need their owners or pack leaders to show them how to behave in a world not built for puppies.

Our homes have stairs, kitchens, doors, many other obstacles and different rules that a young puppy would never face in a natural environment. In most cases, the puppy's natural instincts clash with how humans live.

Puppies need to be taught skills that will allow them to navigate the human jungle to stay happy. This in turn will keep the owner happy too!

Important:

When training with commands and activities, make sure the puppy has not eaten, so he will be hungry enough to want treats. Also, start most core activities in areas without distractions.

Heel

The **#1 command** to teach your puppy is to HEEL. The heel command not only gives you command over your puppy's place near you, but also it <u>quickly establishes you as pack leader</u>.

Teaching a puppy to heel involves walking your puppy, which I suggest you do every day. Take your puppy on a long walk each day and require him to walk next to you or behind you. Your dog should never walk in front of you, because he will then assume the pack leader role. That's your job at all times.

When it's almost time to take your puppy out for a walk, it's first necessary to prepare.

Step 1 – Call your puppy to come to you.
Use the SIT and STAY commands, so the puppy knows to wait no matter what is to happen next.

Step 2 – Wait until your puppy is calm
Step 3 – Place the leash and neck chain on your puppy.
Step 4 – Open the door. This is a good time to teach your puppy to come when you are ready, not when the door opens. Your puppy needs to learn to wait when you say STAY and to not jump through the door just because it opened.
Step 6 – Call your puppy outside to you and make him SIT immediately at your side. You have the leash in a loose hold, because you want your puppy to follow along side you. Eventually you will want to practice walking in no-traffic,

low distraction fields or country walkways without his leash, so he remains heeled when you desire it and not because he is attached to the leash.

A good place to teach the HEEL command is in a large, low grassy field where the single purpose is to walk your puppy with no distractions. You can stop and start easier and teach HEEL to keep your puppy at your side.

Slow down as you walk. Should your puppy walk ahead, give the HEEL command with a gentle tug on the leash to bring your puppy back where you want him to walk.

This is easy correction as your puppy begins to learn to walk closely to you at your side. A key point to train your puppy to heel quickly is to keep this training calm. Your puppy may want to dart away from you or he might get too excited.

Stop. Have your puppy SIT until he is calm. You need to be calm, too, and clearly picture in your mind what it means for your puppy to remain calm as you walk with him heeled to your side.

In all times, you are in control of this walk. When your puppy wants to stop and sniff, give the leash a quick tug and command to heel back in place at your side as you are walking.

You are leading your puppy. Keep that in mind at all times. When your puppy appears to wander from your side to do anything, your puppy is then in control and leading you.

Tug the leash quickly and heel your puppy. You don't have to stop as long as your puppy regains position.

Your puppy needs to learn to keep his attention on you and that anything else is a distraction that the pack leader won't tolerate. When your puppy's head turns away to see another puppy or to observe a distant sound, tug the leash or in more forceful circumstances, touch his neck firmly with the tips of your fingers to get him to look where he should and regain the entire heeling position.

Consistency is important to the success of this training. When you allow one distraction to take your puppy's attention from you, the next correction may become confusing to your puppy. You can teach your puppy to successfully heel while walking with you after just one or two walks. Some puppies do take longer, because they may have more energy or they aren't as socialized yet.

Consider these walks as a way to drain the extra energy, so walk your puppy before you go to work for the day and always before you serve food.

Keep calm and keep your puppy calm as you walk past other puppies. Owners with untrained puppies will work hard to keep their over excited puppies from approaching you, but your job is to keep your trained puppy in your control, heeled, and with its attention on you as the pack leader.

No common activity that you and your puppy will come up against is more important than you keeping control and keeping your puppy calm and heeled as you walk. A heeled walk will train your puppy to keep you as pack leader as long as you walk your puppy properly beside or behind you, and with confidence that you are the pack leader.

Establish yourself as the pack leader

Many owners disagree on the top 10 items a puppy must learn quickly. Lists do vary, but they aren't significantly different except for this one item.

Establishing yourself as the pack leader is possibly the most important lesson you can teach your puppy right away. It isn't difficult to do, but it can be a little heart rendering.

As an initial puppy owner, it is easy to get off course and make the puppy see you as a friend instead of the pack leader. You can have both to your satisfaction, but it is important to remind your puppy every day that you are the pack leader.

Never does this involve any form of meanness, yanking with a chain or rough activity to prove dominance. In fact, it is more about withholding love, affection and attention until your puppy is calm and submissive to you.

When you first see your puppy for the day, do you get wide-eyed and giggly happy? That is a common response most owners have to an approaching, yawning puppy that is wagging his tail faster than you can see it move.

Showing that highly animated love and attention on your first meeting for the day is

one way that you can lose the pack leader badge from your puppy. There is definitely a place for all that love and attention, but not quite at that moment. Stay with me here as we explore why your self-control is important.

Your puppy's mother would naturally train her youthful pup from the beginning and continue to assert her position as a pack leader.

She does this by making her pups **wait** for food. That's one of the easiest boundaries for her to assert and control. She does this in a calm and controlled way. She also sets other boundaries such as her private territory, distance the pups may run from her and other limitations that you will find necessary to assert for your particular home.

Pack leader dogs in the wild assert themselves calmly to other dogs in the pack, but they do that with a confident attitude that includes clear body language. Unmistakable eye contact is not accompanied with a happy tongue wagging.

An important lesson for you to learn is how to communicate that you are always the pack leader that deserves respect. Causing your puppy to wait before giving eye contact and using your love and affection as rewards are powerful ways to assert your position.

IGNORE

Whenever you disappear from a room even for a short time, ignore your puppy for one or two minutes when you come back. Give no eye contact.

Your puppy has a sense of smell a few thousand times greater than your sense of smell, so he knows you are coming before your feet get moving. What your puppy is now watching to get from you is **your eye contact. Don't give it to him yet. Wait a few minutes without making eye contact.** When you're ready to interact with your puppy, use the **sit** command before any type of fun activity from petting to feeding to walking.

SIT

Reaffirm your puppy's obedience by giving him a command, such as 'sit', before any fun activity or interaction. Sit can become an easy command that will get your puppy accustomed to you as the pack leader that requires his attention. You can give a treat when the command is followed, but do not give a treat when it has not been followed. (See the SIT command lesson). Since you are the pack leader, you can require your puppy to earn food, praise, and water by accomplishing a common command like **sit.**

CONTROLLED EXERCISE WALK

Each day take your puppy on a controlled exercise walk. You are in control of the entire walk that is intended to walk off extra energy, keep your puppy from wandering, maintain position, and reaffirm you as the leader.

Hold the lead firmly so that you will keep the puppy at your heel next to you or behind you.
Maintain a slightly more brisk pace than normal, but don't create a constant pull on the leash. A light tug to get back in position or use of commands to heel is enough.

Be assertive, firm, confident and calm in your commands and movements. Do not be aggressive or hurtful.

This exercise is important for you to learn how to do well to keep your pack leader position.

Your puppy is learning that you are the pack leader here, so it must not be allowed to stop and sniff or slow down the pack leader.

You also control where the puppy will eliminate, because you are the leader. There is no territory marking or stopping unless you choose.

Your puppy will have his attention on you as you do this correctly. He will be looking toward you for leadership that he expects. Each day take your puppy on a controlled exercise

FEEDING

Part of being the pack leader is that you make your puppy wait. That includes waiting to eat on a schedule you determine. Puppy feeding must be at scheduled times. The pack leader also eats first and requires the puppy to wait until all the humans are finished eating.

Don't serve scraps of food from the table.
Don't allow your puppy to nudge your hand to get attention for more food. That is your puppy telling you when it will eat.

Do fill the puppy food bowl, and then require the puppy to sit and stay until you permit him to eat. Just because the food dish is on the floor does not mean it is time to eat.

Don't overfeed your dog and be sure to keep all food and water bowls clean.

birth to 6/8 wks	Mother's milk – keep puppy with the birth mother
7 to 8 weeks	Wean to solid food gradually Feed 3 to 4 times a day. Actual amount varies by size of breed.
About 6 months	Begin feeding 2x per day
10 to 12 months (smaller puppies mature faster – about 30#s)	Change to adult food gradually over two weeks. Puppy food can be fattening to a maturing dog. However, abrupt food changes aren't easy for a dog to tolerate without creating a gastric disturbance. Gradually mix in more adult food during the changeover period.
12 to 16 months (medium puppies up to 80#s)	
up to 24 months (large puppies over 80#s)	

Puppies are looking for natural leadership. Your puppy can sense when you don't have the confidence to be the leader. Assert your position by being calm and controlled. Aggressive dominance is not part of good puppy training.

When you choose to do this to your puppy, you are establishing your leadership in as much as what you do as what you don't do.

Either you lead your puppy, or the puppy will assert his leadership over you. That means you give the great love and affection at your choosing and in first response to some job well done.

Did your puppy have food, drink water, or go out to potty on schedule? Did your puppy pick up his toys or sit still or come when called?

To become the pack leader and remain that way, you need to have a calm and confident feeling with an approach that makes your puppy know you are the one to turn to.

After your puppy has accomplished something for the day, then give praise as a reward. This is different from loving playtime fun. You are the one your puppy wants to trust who has the guidance he needs to grow.

Your puppy is watching you at every chance he can to learn what is important to you.

You are the pack leader.

Crate Training

Puppies are den animals and they are naturally inclined to sleep in confined areas. Many owners allow their puppies or young puppies to jump into bed with them when they want to sleep developing a habit that can be almost impossible to break later on in the puppy's life. Allowing a puppy to sleep in your bed with you also defeats your position as pack leader. At the most, let your puppy sleep at your feet, but not above your head.

A puppy's crate should be small and its size should increase as the animal grows. Choose a crate where the animal can <u>stand up, turn around and stretch out</u>.

You can choose a crate that will grow a little with your puppy, because your puppy will grow fast in the coming months. Larger, adult dog crates are available with divider panels that close off space for your puppy. A smaller crate causes a puppy not to relieve himself in the crate, forcing the puppy to leave his home den to go potty.

Smaller crates with enough room for a puppy to move around teach the puppy that the crate is his home and place of rest.

When your puppy is allowed out of his crate, take him immediately outside and encourage him to go potty. Follow the housebreaking section to help encourage him with praise, but always praise your puppy for the job well done.

Be sure to keep your puppy's crate in an area where the family congregates. Many people make the mistake of placing the puppy's crate in an area that has no human traffic. This isolates the pet and makes him associate the crate with being alone. Unsocialized puppies have no experiences to help them understand what to do with people. Keeping them isolated can frighten them, cause them to fight attempts to enter the crate, and create anti-social behavior. (This type of activity may be beneficial for developing one-sided, aggressive guard dogs. This book does not cover that type of training.)

The best solution is to find a spot close to the pack leader or other members of the family, so the puppy is calm and relaxed in the crate.

The crate should also have comfortable lining so the puppy can feel at ease. Wire floors can make paws hurt after a while, so be sure there is a mat inside or something soft covering an area where your puppy may rest.

Owners can start crate training by placing the puppy in the crate for a few minutes at a time several times a day. The time spent in the crate should then be slowly increased. The puppy should realize that the crate is not a place of punishment, but its own space to relax and hangout.

Consistency is very important in crate training. Remain consistent with regular feeding and put your puppy in the crate as regular and consistent training throughout the day. You will have a happy place for your puppy and your housebreaking days will end fast.

Part of crate training and managing destructive chewing is to leave your puppy in the crate when you leave for a short time. Remember, the puppy naturally doesn't want to soil his own home, the crate, so don't stay away too long past your puppy's normal potty time.

Make sure that you remain calm yourself whenever you put your puppy into the crate or let him out. You want the crate to be the natural den of your puppy that he wants to enter and leave when the door is open. Do not associate rewards or high praise with the puppy going in or out, so be sure to wait after your puppy comes out of the crate to be affectionate.

The crate is your puppy's home den. *Never involve this crate in any form of discipline.*

Puppy's Name

Owners should teach a puppy his name early on and condition a specific response when his name is called. In most cases, you want your puppy to
STOP what he is doing
TURN and
LOOK at you when you call out his name.

This can be done by first standing close to the puppy and calling out the name.

Step 1
Say your puppy's name using a very happy tone in order to make this a desirable exercise for your puppy. Only say the puppy's name once.

Step 2

When the puppy STOPS and <u>looks toward you</u>, then reward him. Your puppy may walk up to you, but that is not the behavior you want, so don't give a reward. That action is specific to the training "COME" described later in this book.

Initially your puppy is probably just curious about what you are saying, but the positive reinforcement means he will look again to get a treat. Use high value treats such as cooked beef or chicken diced into 1/4" cubes

Step 3
Let a little time pass so your puppy's attention changes to something else. Call his name again.

Step 4
Reward him immediately as he looks up at you. You want him to associate his name with the treat you are giving him while you are praising him.

Step 5

In one training session repeat the name call-out exercise up to 10 times. Reward him every time he looks at you. Let the session end so your puppy doesn't get bored listening to his own name. Continue at another time.

Once your puppy starts responding properly to the call of his name, when you are close, then start increasing the distance between you and your pet.

Train your puppy to respond properly when you call him from varying distances. When your puppy responds properly at least 75% of the time, then consider your puppy understanding his name. However, continue to reinforce this activity from time to time to keep the understanding fresh. Add this puppy name training into playtime, and when other activities may distract him.

You may find that your puppy needs a close-to-far refresher course before you add distractions. Anchor name understanding well, so the distractions are easier to manage. Simple distractions, such as passing cars or distant noises that turn his head, are good to use for calling his name.

When you call his name during simple distractions and he responds, add increasingly difficult distractions using friends, other dogs and eventually crowds and groups of animals.

My older brother had a German Shepherd years ago that loved to sleep in an upstairs closet. On one of my visits, my brother was proud to show me his obedient and very intelligent dog.

In the middle of a conversation with me, after I had been sitting for a half hour talking with my brother, my brother spoke the dog's name. He said the dog's name in the same tone and the same volume as the rest of his sentence to me.

We kept talking as I heard the dog wrestling around upstairs until he found his way in front of my brother where he received big hugs and kisses.

Leash

Training your puppy how to walk with you and respond to a tug of a leash can make both your future lives easier. Leash training is important because a puppy must learn how to behave or it will act rowdy and feel in control each time it is on the leash. Once that control is handed over to a dog, getting him back under control when he is around other people and animals is hard.

The leash skill is also important, because a trained puppy is easier to handle during a walk or exercise.

Be sure your leash is light weight and the collar thin to not create undue pressure or stress on your little puppy. Many puppies accept a collar and leash in a short time, but others need help accepting it.

The first thing to do with a young puppy that has never seen a collar or leash is to get the puppy accustomed to the collar. Many puppies at this time won't have much difficulty wearing the collar, because some training has already been effective and your puppy is now calm and attentive to your voice. However, there are puppies that get fearful and attempt to scratch off the collar.

Have your puppy calm down in a room with no distractions. Do not make this a big activity with an accomplishment treat. Be calm and a little matter-of-fact about this new activity.

Put the puppy collar loosely on your puppy. Not so loose that it might slip over his head, but not too tight to be uncomfortable and cause itching. Distraction for this first time activity is helpful, because you want your puppy to not even have much attention on it while he considers the training coming up.

In case he tries to scratch the collar off, take some time to comfort him, play with him, and let him play with a favorite toy, so he is distracted long enough from the collar. He will soon become used to the collar and will not feel frightened wearing it.

Later add the leash when your puppy is preoccupied with another activity. Some puppies are terrified of the tug from a leash, so resist the desire to control your puppy by yanking on the leash.

Although you are in control, a frightened or agitated puppy needs to become calm. Treat your puppy gently to help him understand that this is another exercise leading to good puppy habits.

Let him run around in an area of the house with the leash attached to the collar where the leash won't get caught on something.

Caution: Do not do this outside where branches, bushes, toys, garden equipment, outside furniture can get the leash wound up and harm your dog.

Help him learn what the leash is for and give him time to find it part of the training.

When using a leash on your puppy, make sure you walk in front of the animal to show you are in command.

A puppy should walk next to the owner or behind the owner and never in front. (See: CONTROLLED EXERCISE WALK)

Socialization

This is a very important skill and helps develop a calm temperament in the animal. Puppies need to socialize early, so they are not frightened or aggressive during common day-to-day situations. The most important aspect in socializing a puppy is to make as many possible interactions and pleasant experiences during the young days of your puppy's life.

When your puppy gets frightened by a certain event, it may become scared of the object or person for the rest of its life.

So, it is better to make sure the puppy is calm before introducing him to other people and especially other animals. You can invite friends and family over and introduce them to your puppy.

Make sure to include men, women, children and as many different types of people so your pet becomes accustomed to socializing with humans other than yourself. Another good idea is to bring other well-trained animals into controlled contact with your puppy.

Visiting the Veterinarian

Frequent visits to the vet are important to keep a puppy healthy as it grows and through the rest of its life. Most puppies hate going to the vet because they associate the entire experience as unpleasant and stressful.

Puppies need to be taught early on to accept visits to the veterinarians without creating too much of a fuss while also allowing themselves to be examined.

With just a little effort, you can condition your puppy to be accepting of the veterinarian's office visit.

Examine your puppy at home in ways that you think a veterinarian would look over your puppy. As you do this a few times before the first veterinarian visit, the puppy will become accustomed to the first visit before arriving.

Remember, there may be other types of pets in the waiting room. Socialize your pet and prepare for this first veterinarian visit by exposing your puppy to neighbors' pets as long as you trust the pets have had the necessary vaccinations.

Socializing your puppy to other puppies and pets before the first veterinarian visit can ease the excitement considerably. Imagine all those many sensors in your puppy's nose, thousands more than what you or I have, and he is walking into a world that resembles him in many new ways.

Also, take short unplanned car trips so the puppy does not assume that a car trip can only mean a visit to the vet.
Be sure to teach the heel command and the controlled exercise walk under the section about training your puppy to recognize you as the pack leader. In one or two days you can accomplish a great deal of calm and control.

No/Stop

NO or STOP are an important command that need to be taught to a puppy early on in its life. The no or stop command should feel and sound different from the same way you call your puppy's name.

Positive enforcement is a good way to teach a puppy no and should be used when the puppy stops doing something when you say no.

If the animal does not react properly the first time, you can stamp your foot or snap your fingers to gain its attention. Reward it when it follows the command.

Treats are useful most of the time when starting out a new training behavior, but remember to use more praise and loving attention to replace treats as the training becomes ingrained.

Come

Training your puppy to come when called should also sound and feel different from the reaction when the puppies name is called or from the No/Stop.

As you build your command list, it is important to remain consistent. The sound, feeling, and even your body position (ex. hand gesture) can all become the entire command.

Make sure the animal has first learned the skill of looking toward you, when his name is called.

Then proceed to teach him the **come** command. A good way of doing this is standing a couple of feet away and saying, "come" while clapping your hands. Your puppy may walk towards you. Reward him for a job well done.

Owners can also entice puppies with food treats while saying the command.

Keep backing away from the puppy while saying, "**come**" for about 10 minutes as a single training session. Then take a break or stop.

Sit

The sit command is a prerequisite to teaching the puppy the stay command. The sit and stay command together keeps young puppies from inadvertently climbing up on things. Sit and Stay are the commands that prevent a puppy from dashing out the door whenever it is opened. They are those valuable commands that stop your puppy from jumping up on visitors.

Always start a new core command, like sit, in a location with few or no distractions.

The best way to teach a puppy to sit is to hold a treat above the puppy's head, so it has to look up toward the treat. When you do this method right, you won't need to push the puppy's backside down.

Here's how to make your puppy learn to sit:

Step 1
Hold a treat between your fingers and thumb in one hand.

Step 2
Place your hand about an inch away from your puppy's nose as you start to guide your hand up toward the top of your puppy's head.

Step 3
Your puppy may want to lunge for the treat, which means you are probably more than an inch away.

Step 4
As you move your hand with the treat up toward the top of the head, he will watch it and move his snout upward.

As this happens, he will naturally sit in order to keep balance.

Step 5

The moment the puppy sits, use a common treat word you will use for all training when it is necessary. Good suggestions are that you can say OK! or YES! or ALRIGHT!

By using this word, you teach your puppy to wait slightly before obtaining the treat and you teach the puppy that a treat is coming even when it's not visible.

Sometimes a puppy will backup to get a better view of the treat, instead of sitting down. To control that action, move your puppy close to a wall so he cannot back up.

Give your puppy the treat when he sits and say "SIT" in a firm voice. Make sure he does not jump up to grab the food. You want the puppy to sit successfully. Repeat the steps again until your puppy completes the sitting action well.

How to progress:
Your part in this is to use less of all movements, so the <u>puppy sits on verbal command only</u>.

Try the above activity with only your hand movement and no treats visible. Since your puppy has already found success with sit and treats, then this movement will not be difficult to learn.

Give a hidden treat from your pocket as you find success when your puppy sits and you say "SIT."

The next part of the lesson is to move your hand farther away.

Place your hand up to 10" above your puppy's nose just in front but above so he must look up to see your open hand. Then slide your hand back above your puppy's head still about 10" away while you say "SIT." Your puppy will most likely sit successfully. Try again or reinforce the action with the treat in your hand until "SIT" is associated with the activity.

Problem sitters can easily get the idea of sitting, by practicing this command with the puppy's hind quarters close to a wall. When the puppy backs up, he will instinctively sit.

Puppy Doors

Many puppies do not understand puppy doors right away, so it is a good idea to condition them to use the door every time they need to go relieve themselves outdoors.

This type of training will prevent messes inside the house and make life a lot easier for owners.

Puppy doors can be frightening for a few reasons.

One cause of fear is the size of the puppy door.

Is the door large enough for the puppy so he can go out without having to hunch down not to hit his back?

Also, the puppy doesn't know what is on the other side of the door. Sometimes puppies will poke their head out and come back in.

Temperature or weather changes aren't always what the puppy wants on the other side.

The first thing to do is to get the puppy accustomed to the bang the flaps make when the animals go through the door. The sound should not be associated with a difficult event or give him the impression he has done something wrong.

Be positive and happy when you put him through the door so he knows there is nothing to be frightened about the puppy door.

You should also put the puppy through the door every time you take him outside so he associates the use of the puppy door with going to the bathroom. He will eventually go through the door by himself.

Control Biting

Young puppies are taught by their mothers not to nip or bite excessively. Since puppies are taken away from their mothers and the litter at an early age they are not properly taught this lesson and can bite and nip their owners.

One way to stop a puppy from biting is to socialize him with other well-trained animals. Well-trained animals will teach the puppy not to bite naturally.

At home, the owner must be the pack leader and stop the puppy from biting every time he does it. The puppy must trust and respect the owner in order for these lessons to stick.

Puppies that continue to bite are looking at you as a friend and not the pack leader. The distinction is very important.

Sometimes puppies bite, because they are scared and the trust factor helps stop this behavior.

Remember, too, that puppies often bite or nip when they are playing.

A puppy may bite other times when you touch an area that is hurting or injured. I've had animals bite at me instinctively, because I touched an area that had a mosquito bite or some infection under the fur.

How to Conquer Difficult Training Mistakes Every Puppy Owner Makes

No matter how often I train a puppy to do even the simplest task, the training is always different. Sometimes it is fun, other times it is a little exasperating, but the rewards of a well-trained puppy bring much enjoyment for many years to come.

Owners consider the most common factor to be the type of breed that differentiates the training process. Of course, breeds have different levels of intelligence, awareness, calmness, agility, and different abilities for easy training and other factors. That makes the puppy you have chosen unique for your abilities in how you train.

Your puppy is a most resilient animal. Making some mistakes here and there will not ruin the overall training, which is the most feared aspect of most puppy owners. Avoiding the mistakes mentioned below will ultimately save you time and the extra effort that will come from having to repeat similar practices.

While looking over these important areas, think how you can add more benefit to each training session you have with your puppy encompassed with love, compassion and overall consistency.

Not Training Enough

Practice does not only make perfect for people, but it is essential for puppies as well. Once the puppy is familiar with the people around him, the relationship is easily stabilized. The door to learning will open up.

Consistency in training is the key to keeping your new puppy happy and willing to perform the most important responses you seek to teach.

Puppy training is like any other type of study. When you practice regularly and thoughtfully, you get better at it every day.

When long intervals remain between training, your puppy will forget or lose interest in what you have to teach.

Always remember that if your puppy is responding to certain commands, it is important to repeat the training regularly to keep him actively participating. After a particular command or trick is perfected, move on to the next.

Training Sessions are Too Long

Training sessions need to be broken up so that you and your puppy can soak up as much knowledge as possible without going overboard.

Puppy training is about your fun, too. An interested puppy will be happy to learn new tricks and special activities when you have your own interest and desire in the game.

Training a puppy to do new activities that he would not normally be accustomed to requires patience and your consistent desire to see him succeed. Some people call this work.

I find this time with my puppy some of the most cherished moments I will experience with him. He's growing day by day. There may be times I wish he could grasp the concept a little faster, but I look at myself to see what I am thinking, feeling and doing that makes me impatient.

It is impossible to teach a puppy all the tricks in a book in a single day, because he will not only become bored, but eventually he will refuse to take part in the activity.

Responsibly rewarding a puppy is essential. This is why it is important to practice doing one thing; rewarding the puppy and then continuing again later in another session. This does not mean that a training session should not just end because your puppy is failing to show any signs of success. Keep on trying until the puppy shows some sign of understanding and improve on that from thereon.

Keep training sessions short, about 10 to 15 minutes, but frequent throughout the day, 2 or 3 times, as a great way to keep the puppy interested and willing to contribute.

Training Sessions are Too Short

A training session that only goes on for a few a minutes as you decide to give up lessens the chance of positive result. The worst side of short, ineffective session is that you will be training your puppy to expect the behavior repeated. Planning your puppy training sessions is important, so there aren't interruptions that will derail the session. This doesn't mean that socialization won't have interruptions. That is part of the plan, but when training tricks and special events, interruptions make the training unproductive.

Relying on Treats Only for Positive Reinforcement

Do not get this heading wrong. Giving out treats to your puppy is essential in showing that he will be rewarded for actions he performs, but relying too much on it will obviously not get the desired results. There will come a time, when the desired action should be performed without a treat and in a normal setting, which is why the puppy should not be fixated on a treat every time an action is performed. The over use of treats causes your puppy to perform for the treat, instead of performing and identifying the treat as a reward for the action. Look at it this way, a puppy that performs for the treat may no longer perform on a hand command or voice cue that isn't associated with the treat.

Other methods of praising a puppy are useful indeed in this regard. Treats should be part of the process, but not always. Add positive reinforcement variations like playing briefly with your puppy after he performs the required behavior. Slowly, but gradually replacing treats with more praise, play and even toys is good progress that helps the puppy find value in other positive reinforcement besides treats.

Teaching Commands in One Environment

Every puppy should know that it is the command which is to be followed and not the specific environment that causes the puppy to perform.

Simple commands like "Come" or "Sit" should be followed whether the puppy is at the park or at home. This is possible by teaching the animal in a calm and quite environment. After the puppy has the general idea, try practicing with a little more noise around or where noisy, moving people tend to congregate. Going to the park and practicing is also another good way to conquer this common training mistake and will put the emphasis on the command as intended.

It is very important to remember that this training involves socialization. Train your puppy in patient stages.

Repetition of Commands
One of the most common beginner training mistakes is repeating commands with a puppy that is just not willing to learn at that moment. The puppy may eventually get around to acting out the response you want, but when the desired response comes with delay and hesitation, it's time to take a break.

Repeating the same command over and over without the puppy taking any action can turn the command into something else. Imagine hearing one time to SIT. Then imagine hearing over and over and over SITSITSITSITSIT. The command is actually changed and possibly associated with a different act.

Hesitation may also depend on the puppy's nature. As surprising as it may sound, not all puppies are fond of lying down, especially when an owner applies pressure on their hindquarters trying to get them to sit. Some breeds prefer to stay alert at all times. This is especially true for puppies of a more timid nature, since they feel that such a position would have them more vulnerable and unprotected.

Using specific rewards the puppy particularly likes helps the puppy to be more willing to act. However, be sure you are in a calm environment with no distractions and not directly after feeding, especially in the beginning training phases.

Not Enough Confidence

A puppy will definitely know when you are assertively demanding something and when you are begging for it. When teaching a puppy, it is essential to be in a state of confidence that your puppy can sense. Do not be aggressive, but show you are assertive as the alpha leader of a pack.

Puppies are learning what is important in a new world, so they are willing to follow your confident tone and feeling.

Your puppy will take advantage of a show of weakness. It is innate in pack animals like puppies that one puppy will attempt to rule over a weaker puppy. Show your affection for the puppy, but maintain your position as the head of the class.

Consistency of action and feeling on your part is very important to show your confidence.

Plan what you intend to train your puppy today, and then anticipate how you will show your confidence when your puppy wants to do something else.

Breed and Personality

Some puppies are more sensitive than others are. Some may be more willing to perform new tricks and follow commands more easily, while others may see the whole thing as being unnecessary. Puppies can seem like they are constantly in a mood to play, but play is not always considered as having to work for the rewards.

Try to understand the puppy's nature, character and at which times he is most inviting to new things. Puppies that are not too fond of noisy and crowded environments will definitely not give into training session you have all planed out. So keep in mind that every little factor counts to the puppy being open enough to try new things.

Being able to understand how age, size, energy, breed and even history play a major role in a puppy's ability to learn will ultimately benefit your relationship with him and make you a better trainer in the process.

Using Negative Emotions

Being negatively emotional with a puppy never gets the truly desired results. This is what most owners fail to realize as they tend to become angry or exasperated during training sessions with their puppies. Most puppies will begin to avoid any activity that has to do with shouting, irritation or force. A puppy is a fun loving animal and being that way is essential to keeping it active, energized and enthusiastic while wanting to learn newer, more challenging experiences.

Keep all of your actions neutral, whether the puppy adequately adhered to the trick or command or not.

Sticking to basic rules and guidelines is never too hard to do. Practicing with a strategy in mind is the way to go, which will definitely have your puppy jumping for joy. So head out with confidence next time, knowing that you have what it takes to make your puppy the one that makes you proud to be his best friend.

Not Confronting Head-on

Relentless barking and jumping when your puppy sees a rabbit through the window is part of the group of new experiences that will come up. Often pet owners will let the puppy outside to go chase after the yard intruder. With enough repetition, this 'reward' is teaching your puppy to bark incessantly in order to go outside.

Solving this issue isn't pleasant, because you need to teach the puppy that quiet is what will get him what he wants. The next time this happens, you need to allow your puppy to bark without giving in to its noise. According to Stilwell, of the Animal Planet, it's time to use earplugs. "Wait for that silence, and it will come." Stillwell warns that increased barking often comes before the silence, because the puppy is about as frustrated as you are. "That's how you will know it is working."

Too often frustrated owners decrease activity with their puppies instead of confronting the problem issue with more activity. Do you have a puppy that wildly barks and jumps past the leash while walking near a neighbor's puppy? Coordinate a walk with the neighbor who will walk her puppy down the other side of the street. When your puppy sees the puppy across the street and starts yelping, immediately turn your puppy around and continue to walk back to the house. As you're walking and the puppy stops barking, turn around again and continue the walk. Repeat this until your puppy learns that barking won't get him anything and he is quiet while next to the neighbor's puppy.

Housebreak Your Puppy in 7 Days Using These Proven 8 Steps

Puppies are adorable and cute, but housebreaking a puppy can be one of the more troublesome tricks for some breeds. This stems from the fact that potty training a puppy isn't a natural effort in the wild. You may treat them as babies, but they don't possess human nature. More so, what complicates and increases the difficulty level of housebreaking a puppy is the communication barrier. I like to think that while I'm training how to potty outside, that I'm also learning how to speak puppy better.

Below is the eight step plan to potty train your puppy in seven days. The plan is chalked out from lessons learned through personal experiences as well as speaking with other experts who always have new stories to discuss about the foibles of puppy potting training. Follow these easy steps to housebreak your puppy and you too will have clean and fresh smelling carpets once again.

Step 1: Empathize with your puppy

Puppies aren't conniving to defecate in your house just to annoy you. They are plain clueless on what is expected out of them in a domestic environment. For this very reason, you need to understand effective tricks to communicate your message (in this case: housebreaking) to your puppy. So that he/she understands what you are trying to teach him/her.

Step 2: Know your puppy

Depending on the breed and age of the puppy, his/her bladder control would differ. For example: Smaller breed puppies have smaller digestive systems hence would need to urinate more often, whereas puppies of a large breed are easy to train and get better with age. Same goes with age. The younger the puppy, the lesser would be his bladder control. So your housebreaking plan would depend largely on the age, breed and background of your puppy.

Step 3: Focus on building a right environment

One of the most prevalent and effective methods for housebreaking puppies is the crate training method. If you are of an opinion that keeping your endearing little puppy in a cage sounds cruel, then let me clear the air. Puppies by nature like to snuggle up and sleep in a safe and secure place. That's why you must have noticed that even stray puppies like to sleep under a car or in a den. Seldom will you come across puppies that sleep out in the open. The crate method is designed on the same premise - a way to provide safe and secure house for your puppy.

So first thing first, buy a crate for your puppy. Keep in the mind the breed of your puppy and how fast do they grow in size while buying a crate. It should not be too small or too big. There should be just about enough space for your puppy to lay and roll around.

The whole idea is to compel the puppy to empty his bladder only outside. Puppies like to keep their area of sleep and rest clean. When the crate is huge, they would keep two different spots, one to rest and one to eliminate. When there isn't room for them to choose two spots, they will get into a habit of eliminating outside in order to keep their den clean.

Do not leave any absorbent material inside the crate. Always keep a close watch, especially when the puppies are too young.

For youngest puppies, the crate time shouldn't exceed more than 2 hours from the last elimination.

Puppies less than 16 weeks **can't control their bladder longer than 2 hours**.

Puppies of more than 16 weeks can manage for 4 hours.

Puppies between 4-6 months can wait up to 6-7 hours.

Puppies older than 6 months can get by for 7-8 hours.

Pick up on hints and their body language, like, their facial expression, if they are circling inside the cage or trying to get your attention.

It most probably means they need to relieve themselves and are asking you to let them out.

Step 4: Make a schedule

Prepare a daily schedule for your puppy and yourself. Factors to consider while making the plan is nature of work (are you with the puppy throughout the day or few hours in the day etc), age of the puppy, meal time, sleep time, crate time, and play time.

Write down the schedule on a planner or a note pad. Key would be to follow it exactly and consistently always. Just like us, puppies are creatures of habit.

Remember how tough it was to get up at the crack of dawn but eventually now it has become a habit? That schedule change is the similar for your puppy.

Allowing your puppy to eat at any time will only add to your scheduling problems and reduce the acceptance that you are the pack leader.

Keep to the schedule when you will feed your puppy, take him out, play, put him in a crate, and let him out again at the exact same time every day. He will begin to accept the schedule and quickly become accustomed to its consistency.

In order to discipline your puppy, you will need to become part of the disciplined schedule.

On an average, it takes about 5-6 days for a puppy to adjust to the schedule. Don't change the plan of action haphazardly because you will end up confusing your puppy.

A puppy feels the need clear his bladder after 15-30 minutes of a meal. Create an elimination plan with that timing in mind. And not just after every meal, but take him out to clear his bladder after every nap, first thing every morning after waking up and last thing before going to bed.

Step 5: Train the difference between 'Outside' and 'Inside'

A pet owner sighed, "Even when I take my puppy out, he chooses to come home and urinate on the couch"

Puppies need to be taught that they should clear their bladder only 'Outside'. This can be done by teaching him the word 'outside'. Whenever you take him out, emphasize the word 'outside' specifically. Gradually he will understand the difference between 'inside' and 'outside and refrain from spoiling your house.

To be safe use the paper method inside your house. Lay down a few sheets of paper for your puppy to urinate. This is particularly helpful during bad weather or when there is lack of open space to choose a particular spot for your puppy outside.

Step 6: Fix a spot

Choose an area for consistent elimination. It could be in your backyard or some other place where your puppy won't be disturbed while relieving himself. Going to the same place everyday signals his brain and encourages him to rush to the same spot and not go anywhere else. This will dissuade him from urinating inside your home. A place which looks and smells familiar will trigger the memory and the puppy will know the purpose behind you bringing him to the same spot.

Once you take him to his spot, use affirmative and encouraging words like 'do potty, go potty, hurry up' repeatedly. Do not rush, force, drag or nudge your puppy to do his business quickly. Allow him to take his time.

Step 7: Reward and Praise

Every time your pup follows your command and does his business in the right place, reward and praise him immediately. This way he will know he behaved well and made you happy. Showing excitement on your face, using happy positive words, hugging and kissing your puppy are ways to show appreciation. Do this every single time when you see your puppy pooping and peeing at the right place.

Step 8: Be firm, not harsh

Accidents can happen, so don't be surprised when you find your puppy urinating in the crate or on your favorite carpet. Make your disappointment evident immediately in a firm voice using a single command as long as you discovered your puppy in the act of committing the mistake. Use only one command so that the puppy identifies it easily and knows he is doing something wrong.

Reprimand your puppy only when you catch him in the act immediately. Your puppy is an animal, not a human with whom you can reason and lecture at the end of the day for all his actions.

Your puppy may chew a book and carry pieces all down the stairs, but you can't rub your puppy's nose it a half hour later expecting him to understand what all the fuss is about.

Do not beat, yell, punish or use harsh words. It is not only cruel, but it will harm your puppy's mindset. Never lose your patience on your puppy and never treat him in any inhumane manner.

Learning the differences between firmness and harshness, and assertive action and aggressive action is an important puppy owner lesson.

When training doesn't help
A client had a problem and asked, "I have been trying for almost 2 months, but I still find feces and patches of urine inside the house after coming home. Is there any physical reason I need to be worried about?"

It would be wise to get your pet checked from a veterinary doctor to rule out possible infections and diseases. It is quite possible that due to some health reasons your puppy isn't able to control his bladder. If no such problem is found after checks and tests, it would mean you need to start potty training from scratch. This time you will have to be more firm.

By following a proper schedule after considering all the above mentioned factors, you would notice your puppy behaving well within a week. Yes, puppies are smart and fast learners. This doesn't mean a little leeway is possible after a week because there is still a long way to. Just ensure you maintain consistency and patience while potty training your puppy.

While doing this laborious work, be sure to offer plenty of praise and love for the job well done!

Conclusion

In the introduction, I told you about my friend's dog, TIMMS, and how his brother liked to torment her whether he believed it was fun or not.

She never forgot that treatment, and when he would come around, she would hide.

From that experience, I chose how I would treat her. I never wanted to give my friend's dog, TIMMS, a reason to doubt me, or to fear me in any way.

That wonderful dog obeyed me in everything I asked of her. She loved me and I loved her. She never forgot who I was even when I was away for a long time.

When you understand how to create a pack leader relationship and yet still love your puppy with no thoughts of harm, you will create a unique bond with your pet.

Your pet will want to learn from you and want to please you, and not surprisingly, you will feel the same way about this new addition to your family.

Did you get your FREE copy of my book? Just go to this link on the internet and you'll get all the extras as my gift. ($14.95 value)

"How To Care For Your Dog - 37 Proven Lessons"
http://www.m8u.org/PuppyLessons/

www.ingramcontent.com/pod-product-compliance
Lightning Source LLC
Chambersburg PA
CBHW060845050426
42453CB00008B/831